Hours From A Convent

Other books by Emily Isaacson:

Little Bird's Song

Voetelle

The Fleur-de-lis Vol I-III

The Sunken Garden (limited edition)

Ignatia

House of Rain

Snowflake Princess

A Familiar Shore

City of Roses

Victoriana

The Blossom Jar

Hallmark

Hours From A Convent

EMILY ISAACSON

Potter's Press
Canada

© Copyright 2016 The Wild Lily Institute.

No part of this book may be reproduced, stored in a retrieval system, or transmitted by any means, except for brief quotes, without the written permission of the author.

Cover design and interior layout: Voetelle Art & Design
Cover and design photos © alexvav License X by Fotolia.

ISBN: *978-1-300-85248-3*

First Edition: First Printing: 2013 Second Printing: 2015
Second Edition: First Printing 2016

 Published by Potter's Press

a division of The Wild Lily Institute
P.O. Box 3366
Mission, B.C. Canada V2V 4J5
www.wildlilyinstitute.com

Printed by:
Lulu Enterprises Inc.
www.lulu.com
Printed in the United States of America.

Dedicated to the nuns of the monastery

of St. Clare

Now I am still
and plain:
no more words.

To others I was like a wind:
I made them shake.
I'd gone very far, as far as the angels,
and high, where light thins into nothing.

But deep in the darkness is God.

—Rainer Maria Rilke

Contents:

i. Foreword / 11
ii. Introduction / 13

I. Book of Hours / 23
Convent Vows / 25
Biddings / 36

II. Book of Elements / 47
Gold / 49
Silver / 56
Bronze / 63
Copper / 70
Iron / 77

III. Book of Minutes / 85
Poverty / 87
Chastity / 94
Enclosure / 101
Obedience / 108

IV. Book of Seasons / 115
Spring / 117
Summer / 121
Autumn / 125
Winter / 129

V. Book of Days / 133
Awaken / 135
Endure / 145
Relinquishment / 155

VI. Book of Tears / 165
The Crushed Rose / 167
Truce / 174

VII. Book of Years / 181
Love Shall Burn / 183

Foreword

Emily Isaacson, Canadian poet, employs the language of verse as medium in *Hours From A Convent*. Isaacson's love poems are modeled after some of the classic works of early writers including Rainer Maria Rilke and John Donne. The depth of her poetry belays an even deeper sentiment than love, but that of the serenity of covenant, and of the severity in a contest of wills between the earthly and the celestial.

Isaacson takes us behind the walls of a convent where religion constructs an interior model, as vows of poverty, chastity, enclosure, and obedience draw us deeper into the pursuit of the extraordinary life. The life of prayer in the convent is reminiscent of that of a lover and loved one, from the perspective of a young nun. Hidden away in enclosure in the convent of St. Clare, in the mountains of British Columbia, this young sister must carve out her existence with the mystic divine and her place in the world.

The nun desired to serve only her Savior, but her meeting of a young woman called the Madonna of the Streets is drawing her day by day from a life of duty to one of passionate understanding. This young woman causes her to have visions and spiritual awareness of other places, people and times. Her relationship with God is akin to that of a prince and his new bride, deeply telling of his commitment to her destiny.

Dedicated to the calling, the young nun pours out her measureless praise as both created and beloved of her Creator. Her journey into God in hours, days and seasons try the inner world of her intimacy in the spiritual. Her silence mimics that of an unborn embryo, and yet as she plays out the part of each vow, we find her calling to the realm of the mystic divine of all who enter the convent confines. Prayer, as something beyond the curtain and into the holy of holies, is in obedience to the divine calling. Her lifestyle, in search of the Madonna of the streets, her nature and her purpose on earth, is constantly in search of the prophetic to impart revelation over information. She trusts the mystic divine to offer a call, of invitation over worldly seduction.

This is the tale in poetry that shares with those who have readied their souls for a calling and vocation. We devote ourselves to all that heaven requires of us, and leave behind the unwieldy burdens of earth. We participate along with the convent in journeying into the mystic divine.

The Emily Isaacson Institute, 2013

Introduction

Where the sun sets over the city, there is a staircase which remains my favorite place to sit and watch the people pass by. The many lessons of life were learned and revealed to me as I walked the streets of the city, belonging only to God, cold and alone. The whisperings of my soul have spoken in many languages as I revealed the truth of love to those around me. To capture them all, I would need a muse for each, yet I have revealed here in the next pages something of the journey into self and the relationship with the divine as one grows to know oneself in relation to others.

I have walked through many streets, alleyways, parks, and even been invited in to many homes in my journey, yet the worn sandals and miracle moments only speak of the miles I have walked—not of the people I have met, learned from, and loved; those I have cherished, understood, and relinquished. The brokenness I have watched with an open heart, without judgment—and the lessons I have learned in restorative justice. The application of hope, faith, and promise to those in need of rehabilitation was traded at great cost.

There is a place where we move beyond merely educating people to bringing them the healing hope of reparation.

They reach out and ask for answers, yet we must journey with them for many miles before they realize it was this path they wanted on the road to the divine. What we treasure will cost us everything, and what we want shall require the most sacrifice. The hours and days it takes to write a book are equaled only by the months and years of relationship that heals or breaks me to become the truth bringer for many souls.

Somehow I have journeyed long and found many people had many perspectives and goals, ambitions and agendas. Not all were in line with an end of bringing them closer to the resolution of conflict. Yet every able-bodied person seems to have been given a station, a place they belong, where they speak into the lives of those they touch, and care for those around them with the most discretion.

Humanity is the natural flower of love. It emanates the crushed fragrance of God and delves deep into the mystery of survival. Without it, would not exist the emotion and pathos of mankind. The mysterious soul is in no way limited by the burdens of suffering, but rather freed by its bonds of communion with holiness.

The soul is the center of a human being and protects the inner sanctum of the spirit. The spirit communes and is in intimacy with a spiritual being, namely God. God unites the person with others in communion. Communion, in its essence, is a liberation of the limited mind, a straightening of focus. It is the dire opposite of communism. The passion of Christ involved communion in a life-giving way: the complete emptying of one's self unto death. This is the highest end of a human being: to die for another or one's country.

To indifference is the mind callused, for the wells of compassion, like the deeps of the sea, are unlimited and crash onto each new shore with juxtaposed furor. The natural thought is the inescapable future. The cosmos is regulated and regular, unceasing and unfinished, constantly renewing and completing itself. It is designed to be claimed and cared for, to create love and loved ones, both animals and people. To have victory in the literal sense is to have money, possessions, family, and freedom; in the figurative sense, it is to be born anew inasmuch as one commits error.

To be victorious is to delay defeat; for defeat comes eventually and claims us through death. This is why death is our mortal enemy and steals from us our years and our joys. Victory means our antagonist meets defeat, thus we are in a battle and have the deadliest of opponents. Our most severe thunderstorm emulates the clash of battle. It is a display of splendor and power in a warring heaven and we withdraw into cover. We are defeated mortals; we are incapable of controlling the elements. We can only measure and predict them; we cannot stop or delay them.

We need to be victorious in a measured sense, the ordered war against our opponent: the force behind death, decay, illness, and poverty. This is why we work, strive daily to be meticulous, dress and clean, renew and replenish. These opposing forces cause illness, disease, unrest, and violence—they maim us to the good and beautiful so we are disfigured and incapable.

The hope of mankind is to be at some point transformed by metamorphosis into a spectacular and advanced species, not unlike the butterfly. We are designed for expression and the catharsis of the arts. We are made both for dance and football, to intrigue, and cultivate. We hope to live longer, have more, and be stronger. We shame our frailty. And the weak suffer; they need community to thrive. They need others to lend them a helping hand. They need to be spoon-fed. We have hope to grow, to have a futuristic outlook, to reproduce: what antagonizes its purity is not our domain.

In the mountains of the sun, where the field stretches all the way to the rim of horizon, I have been known to pass hours without a particular goal or care, but as part of nature I found that the mystery of birth and rebirth played on my sentiments. There was always a skylark reaping a dive from the heavens, and a silver cloud which a ray of sun illumined, beside the great chronicler of human nature, the earth in all its abundance and gestation.

When someone is born in pain and there is triumph, there is a joy that deepens out of sorrow, and the life that matriculates is not easily divisible. We worship in our pain and it becomes joy. We trade sorrow for something like chivalry, and do our best to help the next person. With the respect that is due women, partly for having furnished their minds with salvation, for having found a purpose and for refusing a bribe, we will trust the love that cherishes to build them a home. And here, at the end of us, we become selfless too, for society bleeds and cries, it makes amends and mortifies the flesh.

When people find each other in the great vast universe, they sense a kinship between peoples, and when they separate, their spirits still converse over many miles. For friends do not happily endorse separation, but endure it with the goal of being reunited. To befriend someone is indeed a gift of selflessness; to protect and cherish a person for a lifetime, is this gift magnified until it becomes the substance of three cords not easily broken.

To create in response to life's road is to delve into nature, memory, and art: in creation there is both the material and the eternal, for we are both mortal and immortal. The material of this life is what we will use to formulate something that will outlast us, into the next generation: that our children and grandchildren may have a sense of destiny, of legacy, and of heritage. The legacy of the divine has proven God's creativity, and left its imprint in us. Each cell speaks of the order upon which the universe is created, with a purpose for every individual in every time.

As a prolific writer, I have composed over twelve hundred poems and songs. Even as a young person, I wrote down my prayers. This time-consuming practice has served to make a writer out of me. I write because I must, and this is my sole passion and joy as well as my tears and greatest frustration.

Where I had nothing left to say, I was truly and wholly dependent on the life of the spirit. When my thoughts and mind would waver, the deep-rooted tree of my spiritual life was the meaning behind the mask I put over human suffering. Something in my spirit ached for more, and made me leave comforts and home to work at the food bank in the town I lived in, to begin to teach the poor. I believed that everyone was equally deserving of education that would improve their quality of life, regardless of their income or social status. It was the sweetness of a heart that was in pursuit of the eternal that was poured out like olive oil.

The ground I have walked upon speaks to me, as does the trees, the sky and sun. What inanimate object does not become animate in the mind of the poet? What nature does not cry of the Creator? What man or woman does not dream of a utopian destiny where sorrow and pain no longer exist? We desire to love, yet must accept the difficulty and hurt this brings over time, in the process of refining our souls. No one is perfect, and yet we desire perfection and beauty, success and power. I have found, while being content with my station and given to write, that many journeys must be taken into the self. The things dreamed of must be gained within more than without. The real power of freedom is to free a man within himself. To be free without may cause the soul to suffer many bondages, to things, people, and money.

I am one to believe I can bring freedom to others in the places I have suffered. I am a healer who relieves harm and disease in those who are hurt and scarred. I am also part of a community of listeners, and each day is an opportunity to engage. Each moment, we may participate with listening as prefect of a universe that speaks. There is a whispering in the trees when the wind blows that calls to the spirit of mankind. There is a need to listen deeper to what nature has witnessed of history and time, of harvest and birth, of brokenness and reparation. These natural cycles of growth, of family, and of history repeat themselves. We learn their lessons again and again.

As a mystic healer and practitioner, I am one imparting the forgiveness of mankind for its ills. I often watch as people suffer, unwilling to come for help. If only they would relinquish, and with empty hands receive the medicine of the spirit. Yet, perhaps in the light of a future where we enter the journey of healing and listening, we will find a truth that will bid us come and leave everything.

What our souls gather as trappings of the body must be abandoned to find the true heaven we seek. The scars we wear as proof of the time we have spent on earth would only profess that we are counted as worthy. The marks of stress and pain speak of our endurance to carry on despite weakness and suffering. We continue despite hardship for a cause we cannot see and an end we cannot know. In all of this, I believe that many will now overcome.

The simple task of succumbing to the beauty of a Savior in each season is a daily focus— like nature, straining for sun and rain in differing times. I am here to remind us of the end goal of our faith: the process of letting go, the conjoining of the divine with our lives, the blood of a Savior, its reparation. I remind the church of its martyrdom, and the profound depth of the one whose martyrdom we follow. The prose-poetry of this book speaks something of the persecuted church. It is a church that can exist anywhere, regardless of buildings or people, members or tithes, and has more to do with the state of the human spirit.

Listen in and gather knowledge of this mysterious truth: the church of today is built on the ways of prophecy. Those who are prophetic instead of practicing their own agendas compose the true church in all its dimensions. Some interpret the times of society, speak in symbols and dark speech—the mystic relation to the spiritual varies with every person—yet some have very real experiences that words cannot begin to express. They may at times leave the practical behind for the transcendent. Perhaps these two cross each other at an axis, where we work in both the vertical and horizontal plane to accomplish our spiritual destiny. At this point of intersection is the cross.

We have no knowledge of what our crucifixion will entail, but we carry bravely on. We walk through the sorrow, sickness, and separation that life brings. Inasmuch as we love we also experience sorrow, and some lose the peace and presence to regrets, pains, and wounding they cannot forget.

On the other hand, to the depth of our sorrow we have capacity to be filled with joy that passes beyond all understanding —that in the end we may know excellence, peace, and every fruit of the rooted tree. Begin, and walk with me now toward the mystic divine.

Emily Isaacson

Book of Hours

Convent Vows

I.

Here we are,
Israel's covenant measured and exact,
timed to each convent prayer:
each mass rises high
through the smoke of incense
as we lead the way
through our vows
minute by minute,
hour by hour,
day by day,
month by month,
year after year,
the seasons sifting
joys and sorrows.

Our band of gold rings our world
with newfound hope—
that your chalice of peace
is a graceful doe in a green.

II.

The alchemy of morning
translated the dew into
music, simple as a lark's trill,
and darting like a shadow
over the fields,
over the roofs,
it disappeared into the clouds.
And a young woman
with long hair,
seeking to become a nun,
disappeared into the convent.

The figure bearing crucifix,
now the Madonna of the streets,
is no myth, her shadow
falling on the old and infirm,
the dying, the diseased—
all reaching toward that one
immaculate hand.

"Salutations from heaven!"
she announced.

III.

You are the one
who covers our heads
as a baby's face
in the sunshine.

We weep our prayers
when you are grieved,
and sing joyfully
of all you have made.
The height of all creation
is you,
your purity and unselfish
desire for unity in us.

We are one
in the ardent circle of your flame,
and it burns to clarity.
Our eyes shining boldly
at our indiscriminate gift
of love—ourselves.

IV.

Genuine women
authenticate themselves
by practice of the art
of cutting the hair
of youth, and elder—
the wise transmuting the lesser,
to far greater gifts,
their hair falling to the floor
and shining like gold vermilion.

Covered in a robe to the floor,
black and white lattices
cloak the garden in measures
of sound and multicolored light
slated, falls to earth
in unshared moments
of ecstasy and damper petals.

Each flower opens
facing the sun,
looking for you:
and you are there
moment by moment
unfolding like we wished for it
a long time ago.

V.

I grew within your mind—
an embryo in the womb
of time, the starry midnight
moments of shared
nourishment and tranquility,
simple tides of an ocean
with salty breath and tattered air.

Your dark beauty did not
escape my grasp
as I held to you
as a lily in the moonlight,
shaded by night,
and blossoming by day
in fragrant glory.

The sweet white smell
sank under the doorframes,
rendered the other
children innocent,
noticing, reticent,
the burgeoning form
of the mother
and her child within.

VI.

I felt birth's first fiery pangs
and push from dark to light,
when I reached to find you
as the warm smile I
had waited for.

You watched me breathe
the first breath,
and took me so carefully
like the delicate and fragile
ivory crèche.

Your milk
is my sustenance,
my hope rests
in your dark eyes.

Laughing, we taste
our first moments:
minutes and hours
that calm and thrill
our poise, to rise
to contemplate,
and bend,
renewed.

VII.

Sight becomes as new as birth,
seeing first your heart, then
the dressing and bathing
of routine,
the feeding of a sweeter milk
than time's first touch—
of berries broached
to woodland floor—
shake them as angels on a branch.

The apple orchard has
but a reddened rouge,
the spires of late spring rise to tulips
red, orange, and yellow as suns
large as lanterns in this land
where seeds are tiny,
black, and plentiful,
and harvest gleaned
in profusion come autumn.

VIII.

The tiniest cry
meets your ears,
and I will find
a measure of music,
a beating of your heart
'till death do us part.

Swaying in the lazy tall grass,
a long haired maiden
with song
wild as the wind, plucking
the seeded dandelions
to blow them for ransom
toward the rogue waves,
to the rambling tides.

An instrument in your hands,
I become the woodwind
like an oboe of Gabriel.

IX.

The pinnacle of afternoon
wafted sunlight through
the slated panes,
the icons I have observed
since my first renaissance
are kept carefully
in the most treasured
parts of a convent
where love is refined
and truth distilled
to pure
and vivid
water.

How do you show
me the way
on this path,
silver and shining
by moonlight,
lit bravely
by saints and legend:
all chanting, they surround me.

I sing of you.

X.

My heart broke open,
and from its hearth stone
a sister took the bread of God,
broken with her careful hands
into pieces.

The warmth of my soul
steeped the tea over the stove,
deep and healing—
then drank the dregs of humanity
with a guilty shiver.

My past was not unformed
in your eyes,
and the land I had known before
was like a root cellar that had
become sterile and empty,
once stocked, now consumed
by envy, jealousy, and greed.

I decided to follow you to a new land,
and never leave you.

XI.

We walked arm in arm
down a dusty road, my skirts
a plethora of colors
noble and bold,
my hair oiled with perfection,
crowned with English flowers,
white roses revealed their plumage
and spilled perfume
over our necks of silver.

The people hung over their gates
and waved valiantly from their horses,
cheering at the sight
of our staple covenant,
bright as the meat of figs
falling from a ripe tree
with its constellation of seeds.

Ruth and Naomi of old,
we traversed from the land of hunger
to the countryside
where the sea winds blow,
where the winds blow in and out,
and from our sectioned window
watch the salt waves.

Biddings

I.

Come, as you are
and see yourself
the queen of islands
beneath your starry gaze.

Put down roots
like a cherry tree in spring—
blossom in season
and send forth warm winds of rose.

Knight the evening:
a lad with horse
who thought to win your hand
and cast his laurel wreath.

Winner of the prize,
you competed in the most arduous race,
steeling your forehead
to the end of happiness and pride.

II.

Peacocks speak of Holy Spirit's love,
their fiery plumage expunging
hate and ire,
draping the ground with their foliage,
bright with melodies
of picture-perfect guardianship
over elements thunderous
with melancholy.

With you, I am at the center
of all that has meaning,
and the life I have desired
is finally my home
after walking for many miles.
The sweat of my brow
and the work of my hands
have brought the fulfillment
of my dreams,
and it is all in you.

But you command me,
and I must obey.
Whatever you ask,
I will do it.

III.

I build my altar of stones
and light its fire.
I am its sacrifice,
an Isaac to its flames.
I will burn
in its fire,
holy and precious
as first love
unless,
what is pure
in God's eyes
intervenes.

Like a martyr
to his pyre,
I stand
in awe
of judgment's
blaze.

IV.

Spirits of a higher nature
mend the rifts
that unspoken
seem to drift
from you to I.

With silver wings they flutter—
back and forth they fly
into the water blue sky.

V.

The silent
drips of a faucet
seem to echo
my negligence
toward your well-being.

I wish my caring
had overlooked
the holes in
stockings:
but I noticed.

I looked the other way
instead of speaking out for justice,
and valiant drunks
laughed in my face,
spewing dark wine.

VI.

You hear me,
chastened in this room
where myth was once
a chariot and rider
climbing toward the clouds.

You speak,
and your words
are a tryst with love and sorrow,
ever-met by diligence and prudence.

A lion and a lamb
dictate our due process.

I touch you again
because you must
become immortal—
as all kings, queens, rulers, and powers
you must make a nation bow.

VII.

An ointment
to a feverish brow,
covering the cold,
feeding the hungry,
clothing the naked,
they are still mine,
and belong to me,
as poverty belongs to great riches.

I pour the essential oils of
eucalyptus, melaleuca, and rose
over a troubled nation
of hurtful words
and broken promises.

If they are healed,
they will rise again—
leaving behind
the trappings of guilt
and pain, like old clothing
ready for the fire.

Burn, nation,
burn to purity;
let the old notions die.

VIII.

Today, there will
be peace in this land.
Today, there will
be justice and mercy.
Today, liberty will
prevail over fear and imprisonment.

For the mind of man
is bathed in a salve
that cleans and cures,
that dreams and thoughtfully wishes,
sparking a new decade
where I shall speak,
knowing of its power.

What I say shall last forever—
as a child who grows to adulthood,
and buries his mother
with the blessing
of eternal youth.

Love shall burn
here like a candle.
I am the candle
of your love.

IX.

Light and darkness
slip through my fingerings
of the grand piano with
a mighty prelude and fugue.

Dormant counterpoint emerges
breathless at its bearings
like Saturn's rings
and Mars's fire.

Play for an hour or more,
with time no factor
in the greatness
of a master.

Teach your skill
to us as spoken words:
not uncaring, not unfeeling,
sympathy in a crystal vase.

The golden primrose teary
with dew at dawn
shall speak its piece
with all due ceremony.

X.

With the gardener
tending his flock of orchids
like a shepherd,
leading them to drink
rain from the sky.

The vale of daffodils:
profuse and bright
yellow, sackcloth pistils,
hidden bulbs underground.

The wild spice winds blow,
tangling the pines,
whispering in the prolific fountains,
pruning the hedges,
battering the roses
bright with militant arms.

When the irises break and die,
when their translucent pale life
ebbs away, no one will say good-bye.

XI.

I, the angel of seven churches
will at long last blow my horn: surrender.

Run to win the laurel,
lest our light deceive us,
and the impermanence
of the natural world
drive us to restrict
what is good
from fear of illusion
or splendor.

The far of liberty creates chaos,
the catching of the imagination
to a harness, to a structured poetic device
precludes minimization
of the divine to mere humanity.
Lest humanity become divine.
Lest a cradle carrying godhood
swipe the stars.
Lest some higher being
or farce charge you with manhood
that would imbue power
to the ritual altar.
I will not hold you under siege.

Book of Elements

Gold: England

I.

The white wine
spoke of an altruistic moment
when it first glistened
as a grape
from the branch of a vineyard;
now it tells sweetly
of a time
when celebration shall be turned
to the bride
in embroidered gown
rose, fleur-de-lis, thistle, shamrock, daffodil:
a wedding to outlast all beauty,
unencumbered by time.

Each town
lays dormant in silence
until the groom approaches
on his steed;
and with a cheer
to light his gallant eyes
and soldier's dress—
royal red—
they wish him live forever.

II.

The solemn ceremony
belayed the hymnal's vast naves,
and ethereal as doves alight or
angels align, one by one aflutter...

She stood,
immaculate in diamond
tiara: immortal as a rose
in summer's light,
time stands still,
and quieter now
the crowd belays her dream,
romance in comely gestures.

Two rings of welsh gold
inscribed with eternity,
shall bind the baited breath
of Jacob's ladder
toward the even celestial spheres.

Four white horses
and a carriage of gilt gold
proceeding onwards
from the cathedral's sacred spires
of Westminster Abbey.

III.

We collected her wish list—
the makings of a princess
in shell-white gossamer,
woven threads,
linen and velvet,
ivory and emerald,
the crown of life
a sprinkling of diamonds
in her stormy eyes.

Bless, not curse,
she reads,
and all will be well with you.
Do you know that
life is at peace in the lowliest hovel
if the Lord's Prayer
be recited in fear of God.

Tidying, making holy
every movement
of the earth and sea,
the spheres still tilt—
contrast the fixity of constellations
with ever-changing
shadows.

IV.

A lightly blown fairy breeze
spoke of our anointing
for we kissed on the ivory balcony:
under the yoke like oxen,
plowing together in unison
through the years of
nearness and separation.
We rose like a wave of sea crashing to shore
and a crowd roared;
like an ocean we were united around
an exotic island of love.

For cowardice now bowed
at chivalry and
our brave faces shone,
salty with tears.

Our refuge is in
the arms of Almighty,
he is our strength
and our fortress.
I lay my head
upon your shoulder.
I am in Almighty.

V.

She was beautiful
and he was stately;
a husband and wife
to keep warm.

Human nature
silenced in mid-stride,
transmuted to gold
through transcribing poets.

The vale of daffodils glinted
like a gold rush in an old valley
where treasure seekers
sat panning by the river.

They shook the rocks and dirt
looking for a shine beneath
the cleansing waters
always seeking after the ethereal.

God-like it shone
in our hair, in our eyes,
heir and heiress of a triune
dream: to have a king.

VI.

Children at the palace
climbed on the white ponies
under the white-gold sun:
still and ever-trembling,
led along, turning their fears
to medieval knights and ladies.

Children asked to learn
and be tutored in understanding,
first learning the manners
that mind grace,
next the making of cream lace,
the books of law
and regulation of order.

Children sat seeking milk and honey
in the cathedral of the promised land,
sang at the organ's first bold note—
we are with you and in you;
all things stem from you.

Underneath us are
your everlasting arms,
and the blood rose entwined
the gates of paradise.

VII.

We walk hand in hand,
devoted leaders
of a human race—
multi-national and tepid
over the entire globe,
seeking the way.

We speak at gatherings
of one or a thousand—
of the moments that make up
the memory of a people,
that show the way through
the terra-cotta desert
like a cloud or a pillar of fire.

We sleep beneath
the stars in a watery blue ocean—
of the dreams that make men brave
and leave the women they love for war.

We walk down the cemetery pathway
leaving it all behind—
owning nothing on earth,
yet King and Queen
of everything.

Silver: Canada

I.

Your sea was a satin maiden
lashing against the rocky shore;
silent as a muse at high tide,
brimming with tears at nightfall.

Your tide was a wild Madonna,
the shells in her seaweed hair,
white pearls, sewn like dew
over a manicured lawn.

Your beach collected the
ocean's fury, bleached driftwood
here and there,
scattered crabs and hermit homage.

II.

Your stream was a woman
rejected by modernism,
who tended the cold with silver hair,
and reached out over the wood
like a mist, to water each new and living thing.

Your river held the perfume
of summer, a crucible
of apple trees and lilac,
red and purple flowers and fruit.

Your ocean netted the fine fish
to roast over the fire of
human suffering,
welcoming a messianic figure
in the stillness of sunrise.

III.

Your forest was bountiful
with red berries and fern bracken;
deer and fox, bluebirds and bear,
the tumbling crystal stream
filling the glass pitcher with icy waters.

Your meadow sang
in the heat of July
after the heavy sun patterned
with brocade the melting flowers
in the lush grass, with new lime shoots.

Your mountain played its clarinet:
the wind in the evergreen,
its flute, dapples in the rippling brook,
its trumpet,
summoning the noon from heaven,
its horn, laying low
the valleys after the wind.

IV.

Your window had a gentle
candle's glow in its panes,
shielding off the fright of monotony
and nurturing the spoken word
into nouns of prophecy.

Your chair sat in a tangled garden
high-backed and resin wicker
memorizing the verse of the masters
with a steaming cup of peppermint herbs.

Your evensong resounded
like the pillars of time
rising pure and true
beneath the shadows of the night.

V.

Your battle was fought on a final front,
the fight to the end
for your life or mine—
the witch or the prophet will
take your life or spend it for glory.

Your mail glowed with silver shine,
a truce of metal valor
echoing in eyes grown dull
with feverish intent
to spare one's own life,
instead of fighting
to man's dying notion.

Your fleur-de-lis
to raise our arms and heads once again
was a revelation sword
raised for inner dominion
where all kings go—
where kings go to war.

VI.

Your hymn was a hand
reaching to heaven,
a song sung with purple lips of cold
seeking a warm and crimson fire.

Your prayer taught me how to pray anew,
knees bent, hands clasped
murmuring the endearing things
to God that separate his children
from the heathen dressed in rags of no grace.

Your church was a well-dressed woman
who had once worn a veil—
tranquil and serene in every season,
reaping the fruit of time,
bearing the irrevocable vow,
setting her house in order
for the return of her prosperous husband.

VII.

Your dream
was to live forever,
to find immortality
in eternity's last hour;
and minute by minute,
the clarity of colored panes
under gothic spires rang out.

Your verse
was both staid and solemn
in a gold-rimmed hymnal:
counting the days
as precious seeds
to grow a radiant harvest,
counting the seasons
as the means
to water and grow
wisdom.

Your child
played in the sunset meadow,
his trumpet did taps at dusk,
his castle rose, fearless and true—
and he saluted the entrance
while you bowed.

Bronze: Scotland

I.

The Scottish bagpipe
gave its sonorous edict—
what you told me in the beginning
would heal the wound.

The player wearing a
dark green kilt,
its promise
bearing down on
a row of students,
weary from journey,
as I too have grown weary.

They would wait out the years
to the final test,
and with an outpouring of sudden
knowledge
gain entrance to academia.

Many wait to
enter where
I am now standing.

II.

The fiery dust of the thistle,
its roadside fury and dormant purple
flight, national flowers
of people who had given up only to try again.
To make life fit as clothing
they had outgrown as children.

What I love about you
I have never outgrown,
but fitted and re-fitted
through the years
to match the character
of your true love.

When a person's strength
has been sapped,
their energy deteriorated,
no longer strong but frail
on the inside,
I know the exactitude
that restores:
the renewing of the young sap
to kindle re-growth
in just a word,
a single remedy for pain.

III.

We walked along
the path of the Saint,
our friendship, supple
and wandering through
the air of old wood
and ancient pasts.

When you speak, I listen:
I am both careful
and afraid.

The moor beyond
these walls speaks
in a multitude of volumes,
in colors that stay the mind
to witness both God
and the people of this country
I have come to love.

IV.

The minutes
of winding and unwinding
the capital thoughts I once had
for new ideas, occupations,
and interests
makes my mind
learn you
in a way that
I will never forget.

A flexible thread
began its continuum,
to count the moments
in God, in innocent song,
the holiness of another's face,
the sacred mother
of us all.

We were all reaching for
the best in life;
and you had arrived
with thunderous
resolution;
we relinquished
our ovation.

V.

Enduring as the gray seas
lashing offshore
I drank my coffee
as the day began to
grow cold,
watching you write.

Now I see you, bent
over a long wooden table
practicing
what you would say,
how you would be
so as to relay
your studious adulthood,
your coat of arms,
your noble family,
and your country.
Your tentative head
blew a whisper
in my direction
and I paused.
Something about you
made time captive—
your prisoner in a dungeon—
made the sun stand still.

VI.

The coat of arms
was of oak and acorn
weathering on the dry earth
like the hill song of sage
stretching forever into the distance.

My hands were fine and
my graduation cap
sealed my education with a tassel
I entwined with my fingers,
like a musician fingering an ornate
instrument.

The books of art history
and antique civilizations
piled on the coffee table,
were eloquent of foreign
peoples, paintings
and museums
where there was no dust,
only parchment memories
and mementoes,
fossils of
vintage clothing,
and priceless artifacts.

VII.

The fashion of a real woman
walked down a flashy runway
exhorting watchers
and captured forever
in a see-through skin, sheer
black and the light shimmered.
A medieval galleon
set sail for a far-away port
in a gust of tropical wind, and only
one was the captain of its mast.

Bright-eyed,
never growing weary
taking each moment
as a memory
for a people's glittering crown.

We danced, and
each shadow that plays is mine,
like a grand piano echoing
the saxophone in a jazz club,
and I stand at the salute
of a long row of soldiers
in royal dress.

Copper: Ireland

I.

I stand and shake the hands
of everyone who greets me:
in a long line of well-wishers
there are many bouquets.

The multi-colored aura
of dresses and hats,
paisley and perfume,
made me shield my face
and the light respectfully
adorned me from head to toe.

My head is bent in prayer
that I would be grateful,
diligent,
fleeing cowardice—
entering the
daily battle
to win your favor.

II.

Where time would heal,
we now see a future
where there was only strife
and anguish—
gloved hands
reach for Ireland,
decadent in shamrock green,
believing in reconciliation,
bettering the lives
of the youth
and children,
holding hands.

I rise from the bitter death
of war
and blood
to take you back
like an estranged wife
who now weeps in sorrow.

III.

Piece by piece
I put the puzzle back together
so I could again see
where we should be
comrades
on horseback, line by line,
in duty
to a similar fate
and two nations
hand in hand
where we stand before God
for our country.

It was reminiscent of
a pastoral symphony,
yet unplayed.

The clouds rolled by
in blue and white sentiment;
I was a prince and like a shepherd,
tended them—
white sheep,
counted them with care,
bent with my crook
to lead them to drink.

IV.

At childhood's beginning,
you knew my name
when you called me,
and no one
had ever said it before—
I remember you now
from my youth,
your wise eyes,
your calming temperament,
and homage
to common sense.

You were under God,
and I see you unadorned
where we hold hands,
walking in the green
of the next field,
where fire-flowers
bleed red
in profusion,
with neckties of white
skirted by the falling night.

V.

When I call someone
with the eye
to announce in grandeur
their supreme importance
it's Ireland's misted morning
lying low over the
dark rugged hills.

The song
rings and grows louder
creating in us
a new moment
where the truth can
be found when our eyes meet,
and it resonates
in both our past
and future.

The truth is that
we will never be parted
and our silence will
almost seep
louder than words
as we contemplate
our destiny.

VI.

Where once
we played as children
in the sand,
now as youth
we have not parted
and we are strong
to fight in
allegiance.

Only in love will we find
our home
is side by side,
and the dark froth of hate
will dissipate
like thunder over the sea,
after shaking its mantle
of hostility—

Of why things
could not be separate anymore,
like a lover, unspeaking to his loved one
for many years;
until her thirst became a drought,
a million children
begging for water.

VII.

I wandered and no wanton grave
drew my name like a lot:
the simple vestment
gesturing the scarlet wine
to my goblet,
pouring the blessing
on my family and their youth.

We will never forget
our devotion to
each other
through the dark years
of rebellion
would end
at such a splendid table,
rich with the
feast of nations
reconciled.

It is only because
I touched you
and from so close
that healing became
imperial to everyone.

Iron: Wales

I.

From our garden of daffodils
we collected armfuls
of bloom,
decorated every room
with joy,
and sorrow fled,
the laughter of a home
filled each vase
to overflowing,
ricocheted off the walls.

The Easter cross
was carried through the streets
followed by the devout
on foot, chanting
in the sunrise,
and the sun rose
clear and bright—
yellow as a vale
of daffodils in Wales.

II.

The song wafted here and there
glanced off the bright early
brick facades,
deliberated on the stone,
enlightened the mason work,
imbued a transcendent
denouement, stragglers humming
a solemn prayer
as the line faded
away into the distance.

I mounted my chestnut mare
and we followed the gray
cobblestone streets
to the edge of the village.
The countryside lay stretched out
before us, and the light of morning
riveted each valley and hill,
green and stone,
to the edge of the horizon.

The song lay dormant now,
only echoes in the streets
belayed its passing gift
and tenuous resurrection.

III.

I galloped on my horse
into the crevices
and the heart of the countryside—
where story hides,
and love congeals,
wary of a victory,
breaking on the peals
of time.

I made you a promise
I would someday return;
now I will find the meadow
that leads to you.

Your lips spoke the words
silently
when you knew
I had chosen you—or
who's gained my soul.

Shall I be one to attain heaven
and forget the poverty of earth:
I will never forget,
surely as the morning rides
over the fields of darkness.

IV.

Your glossy mane
was as the earth
in which to grow a seed
come spring.

Your delicate memory
remembers each note:
and the chorus sings,
while the stage
relinquishes its applause.

The stone wall where you sat
in childhood
has a spray of apple leaf,
and reddened fruit
overhanging your books.

And you read each word,
a treasure seeking
guest to each hovel
and its heroine.

V.

All hands
were stretching
to touch you,
strangers reached out,
and the sea parted
as we came,
a path of dust opened
on the ocean floor
and the faithful
followed us through
beside
the wall of salt and blue.

They are our children,
a nation
of legend and myth,
a Madonna with child
who dances by the fire.

Whatever is diseased,
they will heal;
whatever is accursed,
what has been left outside,
will be surrounded
and brought back to gold.

VI.

The alchemy of sovereignty
came about through
the thesis of true love,
and doctrine of blessing for cursing.

We transmuted the baser life,
with its evils and impurities,
into gold and the riches
of the eternal.

We took stock of our
storehouse in heaven,
and counted its worth:
filled with silver words
and golden moments,
with flowers of love,
and a fleur-de-lis of truce.

My rose was your blood,
and my thorns
pained your brow,
painting a stained glass
cathedral of worship,
where my hymns
rose clear and true.

VII.

To achieve what is forever
means we are not of this earth,
but citizens of a greater country.

Patriots of Wales,
I therefore announce to you:
take stock
of your past, present, and future;
sow to reap a harvest of plenty,
that you may be rich in the things
that money cannot buy,
that your families
and hearths may prosper
with both comfort and healing,
so truth will be your staple
and honesty your upbringing.
Expunging that which corrupts,
ignoring that which distracts,
turning from that which is evil—
finding in humility
the leadership of a true
home and country.

I beseech you,
follow me now.

Book of Minutes

Poverty

I.

The simplicity of
sunlight when I am alone,
and the joy of togetherness
mark my world,
when perfection
is out of reach,
and performance an act;
before the light,
there was the night
and my unformed
body was in need of you,
like I need you now.

You once observed me
in contemplation:
I was the muse of time,
the dark-haired beauty—
too prosperous to give it all,
and leave it all behind,
but the convent was destined
to become my world
instead of fear and self-doubt.

II.

When I am poor,
I will trust in you.
When I am hungry,
I will eat of your table.
I am not afraid anymore
to work, and work hard
day after day, hour after hour,
minute by minute,
for my sustenance
to participate in this life
with you.

Your lamp lights my way.
You brighten the path
through the wood,
where murmurings
and shadows are only
the beating of my heart,
the fluttering of my lungs,
gasping for breath.

Every cell longs for you,
thirsting, as I reach for moss,
berries, and roots
to steep over the fire.

III.

The woods have hidden me until now,
but like a night bird
flying into the open,
I face the light to find
my life's purpose.

You are my treasure,
and the one desire of my heart;
you are my obsession—
and I believe that I
will one day see you
as you are.

What is poverty,
than the renunciation
of money and wealth
for a chastised life
of work with no reward.

Yet, I see your face
so close to mine;
your heart beats
in my very chest
and I sleep
in the depths of your love.

IV.

I am only as poor
as an unborn child
sleeping in the womb,
where I can hear your voice.
I will remember you
and kiss your hands.

We cannot be distant
but are as close as earth and
metal, wood, and water,
both needing and blessing
each other's worth,
and the fire consumes us.

There is one place
where I am found,
and it is in Almighty.
He is my one source of life,
my home, and all things, outlasts.
I will not be buried in the rubble
when my earthly home fails,
but will find myself purified
in the fire of martyrdom,
seeking what is deeper than words.

V.

My poverty
has become the words of nations,
the wealth of many lands,
and my people are rising
to recover their country
from dictators and thieves.

They will never forget
that renaissance is born
of spirit, not flesh,
that anarchy of the human soul
leads to destruction and violence.

I will start on my journey
into the divine;
there are friends
in this neck of the woods
who are not afraid of the dark,
but hang out the moon each night.

I will yet find my way
to a home of plenty,
where the table is set with food and wine,
and my children are glad
at each new day.

VI.

How is it you are so close
to the poor and needy.
Their reward must
truly be in heaven,
when they give thanks to you
for adversity.

You will always be my destiny,
the one I search after
for many hours, days, and years,
and when I find you,
instead of wealth,
I will hold to you and not let go.

What you have
is worth far more than I could pay
in this cold land,
with long winters and
dry summers.

But carry me home
to that one eternal place,
where I rest my head with you
in the fine mansion
of eternity's light.

VII.

The beauty of the night
rises, a woman
with twelve stars,
and her portion is a son
born not of this earth
but of heaven.

From her, healing flows
to the nations,
rivers from the throne
of the Most High,
and his sacrament.

May I never want,
but may my heart be satisfied
with the good things she bestows.
The sheep of her pasture
do not hunger or thirst,
but are led to drink.

The shadows move like wings,
and the angelic host
surround and protect her;
her heart is a sculpture
in fine marble called La Pietà.

Chastity

I.

When I reach the black gate
and it is locked,
I know only one has the key;
and when he bids me enter
it will be to a home:

I will find a hospitality
that grows with years
and character;
the faith one has in purity
is without price.
And so I have great confidence
that we will walk to the end.

The fields were tinged orange
with the light of morning,
and the farmers rose to tend
to their livestock,
the channels of the river
wound their way across the
countryside to water its fertility.

II.

There was a maiden
that spoke her beautiful thoughts
into prayers,
so they would rest on us
indefinitely.

Her hair was carefully
brushed until it shone,
and her dress was
starched and clean,
without tear or stain.
Her skirts were the color
of new-mown hay.

When the moon, set low
in the sky, at sundown
riveted the night
into flame, and the stars
burned like candles,
she made soap from lye
until it burned her hands.

III.

She dipped beeswax
to form pillars
that would burn
in her windows at dusk,
to welcome the traveler.

She fed and clothed the poor
who came to her
begging for a meal,
she dressed them in frocks
and put shoes on their feet.
They began to sing and
the entire household rejoiced.

When the company sat down
to eat, it was the bread
she had prepared on the table,
and the butter she had churned;
the vegetables, from the garden
she had tended, all were
evidence of the work of her hands.

IV.

Her house is built
on the premise
of a future
that will promise
to repay her.

For she has spared
nothing to those
who go hungry,
and poured water
for those
who are thirsty.
They drink deeply.

Let our chastity
be like the work
of a young maiden
whose hands never tire
of those in need.
She is generous and kind-hearted
without fear of harm.

V.

When I build virtue
from chastity,
you are the maker of this house,
the golden rule
that stands for eternity.

We are statues
in the English dusk,
the last sun's rose
darkening to shadows
waiting for twilight to close
for a night
permeated with starlight.

Bold and purple,
royal as the last day,
this evanesce will
recover what is dispersed,
relinquish what is lost,
and calculate what is saved—
person by person, counting its means.

VI.

I will prepare
for my wedding
as a bride in the white
of snowy mountains,
bathed in goat's milk.

My forehead is oiled
with rosemary,
because it stands
for faithfulness;
my hands are
calm with the balm
of eucalyptus.

Clove and anise
oil my dark hair
to shine in the light,
and I am centered
as a queen in a
palace of stone
ramparts.

VII.

My heart beats
with thanksgiving,
and all my attendants
are here with arms filled
with the flowers of youth.

My nation and my people
surround me,
as a wood surrounds
a new fawn,
and its youngest steps
are toward
its mother.

But I will drink deeply
of this new world,
carrying out
the vows I will pledge to you,
wearing the ring of purity
in Welsh gold on my hand,
bejeweled in a diamond tiara.

And I am true to you:
I will not forget
what I have promised.

Enclosure

I.

My solitude goes deeper
than both mortal and
earthly beings,
as I pray into the stillness of dawn
with each new day.

I will never forget
the quietness of a new embryo
in its mother,
the gestation of
hours, days, and months,
the living and breathing
of two spirits in one.

II.

Everything stopped still
to listen in on
your dream,
and it grew in me,
with a fertile home.

A gestation of light
and insight
saw the way to birth.
And the pangs of silence
gave way to the focus of pain.
You were the husband of this vision:
you will see it through.

III.

I am lost without words,
I am here in silent
contemplation,
breathing your life,
knowing your touch.

I want everything
in me to cry out to you,
deeper than words;
so my solitude
is consummated
by your presence
and your spirit.

IV.

When stillness
rests in my arms
like a young child,
I am at peace
and the war has ceased.

What was built on violence
has proven its destruction,
and instead we sit in a circle
with a talking piece
to understand the waiting
before each person
gains permission to speak.

V.

When the absence of words,
the dance of emotions,
and the guarding of silence,
with enclosure—
like a virtue—is seen as weakness
we fail our humanity.

We hasten our decay,
our hurry toward oblivion,
when significance is not gained
by the things deeper than words.
The human touch
knows how to intersperse itself with words
as in the planting of a garden with flowers.

VI.

Each planting of a thought
from the spiritual
life of Christ into my own
is in dedication to the preparation
I have made so that its roots go deep.

Where my soil is rich and dark,
there is room for the life of God to grow
into a harvest. Many shall eat of its
fruit, and the firmament
shall water it with rain
and warm it with sun—
so that its life does not fail.

VII.

There is a way
of life divine
in the unspoken meanings,
in the gestures of care
and the enclosure of night.

Your holiness purifies my
mortal life,
as the sacrifice of St. Clare,
who left her family of nobility
to live as the poor;
she shut herself into the church
and founded the convent of
the Poor Clare's upon this vow.

Obedience

I.

I will not wish for anything
except to obey God and save a people
in prayer from domination and despair
to freedom and liberty.

There is a chance that we have not yet
died inside or given up the spirit to fight,
but will recover our force,
and that of supreme love.

Those who excel in music and art
sing as nightingales
in the dark,
a song in the night.

II.

Those on whom inspiration falls
will know the divine
gift from heaven:
that the spiritual life will not perish.

They that seek after
what cannot be bought or sold
will find the truth
belongs to those that witness.

The gold that does not grow dross,
the silver that does not tarnish,
the bronze that keeps its shine,
and iron that shall not rust.

III.

All these things call us to face
the throne of love,
with our most menial attempts
at kindness and charity.

We are at once
both leaders and followers
in prayer,
from others and for them.

We are quiet,
we bow our heads,
and cannot hear your answer
unless you draw us near.

IV.

We wait in silence,
hands outstretched
toward the heavens
looking for rain.

We wait for your holiness
to consume us,
your fire to fall,
burning us to purity.

Light our candle, dimming,
burn our hearts with love,
take us for everything we are
and own, for it is all yours.

V.

You have taken me
into the holy of holies
where your deepest heartfelt
presence leaves me overawed.

You have brought me in
to make the sacrifice
before you, that of my greatest
love and timid fear.

I bow down before the altar,
I follow your exact instructions;
I do not falter in the work
you have called me to do.

VI.

From the invisible to visible,
choral the stars—
lead the way
across a great divide.

And you are the invitation:
what I hear when you call
is like the whispers
in the night to young Samuel.

Train me like a priest.
Let me hear your voice—
I will respond,
I will answer.

VII.

I pursue you from a long distance
with only dreams
for evidence
that you exist.

Like Moses,
mine is a healing mantle—
fiery and burning
like a bush in the desert.

Here I am.

Make me your servant
before the nations.
Make me your chalice
before the wine.

Book of Seasons

Spring

I.

O pristine spring!
Thy pensive cataract erupts
with rushing sweetness
from deep wells, forward
streaming through valleys
unhindered:
the waters, sylphs of silver
through the pines,
glancing the mountainside with bloom,
each wild rose deferring the sacred
to a rising prayer
like the first gleam of sunlight.

I wandered on
like man in a dream,
my mind loaded with cares—
now climbing to an altar
made of rough stones
and sacrifice—
to lay it down.
What once was mine
is yours forever.

II.

The forest closed around
my oblique figure,
bent over the place
of my centuries old
vice:
the wanting and desire,
traded for rest in you
and contemplation.

New life consummated
the mountain
where fawn roamed
with deer,
and rabbits scampered
into the thicket.

New hope embroidered
itself on the cloth
of my soul,
a monogram of eternal
worth, of the dedication
of women to restore
and men to reunite.

III.

Over the spring field
the darkness crept,
and from my vantage point,
high in a tree,
I saw singing, an oriole,
at evening's end.

She sang in verse,
as if eternity were tomorrow.
She flew into the hedge,
and twittered there,
as I drank the last dregs
before the night.

I descended from
my lookout to the forest floor,
sought my way home
by beginning starlight
and behold, the oriole sang
as brightly
as if the sun shone in full day;
and whispered in my ear,
of her life—free,
without a care,
save for the berry and the worm.

IV.

I tried to catch a firefly
to light my way,
but it flew into the air,
escaped my grasp,
pin-wheeling here and there.

Turning planet,
with beings great and small,
measuring an adagio
of songs and chirps
from each bird
that flies by day;
and the forest meadow
between two mountains
that part,
as if the sea for Moses,
and we,
people of the wood,
on foot pass through.

The dividend of this world
is brought to us in season,
where we are sharers of
the promise of new life.

Summer

I.

The summer came by noon
before the tide
crashed upon the shore,
reminding with each wave
of the fury of God
beneath the moon.

The heat warmed the sand,
melting the sins
of the days of youth
into a silent sonnet,
where love was not second best.

The salt made my lips
taste euphoric,
promising substance
in afternoon,
and carriages with babes
paraded by.
They smiled and waved,
and knew the best of life
was yet to come.

II.

I turned to the warm wind,
and faced the salty tide,
reasoning with the sand
on my feet,
and the grey-green waters
sweeping the neck of shoreline.

I wore the flowers of the field
like a garland,
a dress of eyelet,
and its white and green
delicate hem sutured
the skirt of my being.

I had been waiting here
for a long time,
refreshment for my soul
always just out of reach,
so I held out my hands
in worship.

The butterfly and the nightingale
entwined their colors,
day and night,
spinning toward the sun.

III.

The water has been poured
into my soul,
without reprimand
or stale consequence
to unspoken vows—
my covenant with truce.

It streams from on high
where the source never
runs dry, but gives
life to all who are near
to the fountain of youth,
stemming from
the city of pure gold.

In the hands of his people
the light is dispersed
to each candle,
and the soul of each follower
becomes lit from within.

My light is lit,
never to be extinguished.

IV.

The summer stole my heart
beating my kindness
like a lover
dressed in woodland
clothing, with a heartbeat of warmth,
yet cruel and insolent,
needing rain
before the dry season.

I ran in fear,
isolating the miles of misery
of warped wood,
pounding the floor
with bricks
to lay a new foundation,
building a new home
with eaves of safety,
and purchasing for my wounds
a truer Savior:
a hearth where my fire grew bright,
as my dulled eyes took flight
with the birds rising
to roost in the night.

Autumn

I.

The storm of autumn
whips the colored trees,
stirs the sunset leaves,
demands we run for cover.

Under the eaves,
the fire is lit and the hearth is warm
as my ever-beating heart.

The clouds mass overhead,
and the rain soaks the fields
deep in harvest hues,
neck-high in corn
sheathed with green.

The apple orchards swell
with juicy bounty,
shiny red and green fruit, picked with care.

You picked me before time began,
and set a place for my heart
in this retreat, high in the mountains.

II.

The last light streams
through the trees,
red and gold,
unlike the vivid hues
of a mighty cathedral.

The notes of setting sun
resound, unlike the organ
in its mighty naves,
the sound of choirboys
drifting skyward.

We sit, you and I,
eager to embrace
holiness and youth,
for as long as they walk
hand in hand.

For a better purpose here on earth,
I would wait a long time
beneath this dome,
asking of heaven for reprieve.

III.

We will be lead by the divine
into all mystery and knowledge,
reaping the best of the harvest,
skimming the cream of the milk.

Nothing will ever separate us
in the heart of each mystic season,
tied firmly to the heavenly realms
rooted in the earth below.

We are practical and love learning,
and the wisdom of intuition
is our mother-guide,
making us sure-footed on the mountains.

We are well-spoken and reap riches
of the mine of truth, jewels of poets,
and clothing of kings,
making us pearls of the sea.

IV.

When the winds blow and the ocean assuages
with its shells and stones, its roar of thunder:
I find you here, collecting the moments
and the memories; you run on the beach
in old jogging shoes, you sit on the porch swing
and watch the maples turn to auburn,
you eat ice cream in the park
where mothers walk with their children,
and the leaves fall, a mosaic of flagrant color.

Who would have guessed
you would put on your best dress,
and walk forward to take the honor
to represent the unfortunate and hurting,
that the flowers would be laid in your arms.

Someone else does your hair now,
someone tells you where to go;
your schedule could burgeon—but you prefer
to sit in the simple chapel to pray
rather than the vast cathedral,
and remember that life passes day by day,
and these are the days of the innocence.

Winter

I.

The pale light has entranced us,
taking us captive to the wintery boughs,
the cold solstice, the blue river,
and the mighty frost, icing the windows.

The snow paints the sky
with delicate intrusion,
each flake reminiscent of a tree
with both roots and branches.

The hibernating creatures
have all disappeared under the snow.
The berries are stolen by the birds,
red and white.

The holly tree is bright adorned,
standing proudly, never scorned,
with glazed red and green,
perfect for the mantelpiece.

II.

The mist hangs low over the mountains
where the snow blankets every living thing.
The love of God is like a threshold
where we may enter and come in.

We stack our boots at the door,
leaving the cold outdoors
for mugs of warm tea, biscuits,
and eiderdowns.

A warm family is the gift
of winter; like cider
simmering on the stove
is the heart of longevity.

The offspring of the wise
bring home provision
in each season, and in the cold,
are like the warmth of a glowing fire.

III.

The glittering gifts
rest beneath the tree this Noël,
the cards from friends and relatives
make merry on the table.

We have in this way,
a connection to the times
when they were near,
and sang with us carols bright.

We gather the memories
of Christmas past,
a plethora of poinsettias
to welcome the season.

The tables of this country are set
in red and green—oranges and nuts, a side note,
reveling in the roast turkey
and chocolate truffles.

IV.

The wide arc of snow
measures my silence,
the footprints behind me,
the only evidence
of a presence here,
traveling on and on.

My face, cold and rosy
tells of a healing
of the old ways
for new health
by foreshadowing
both a cross
and resurrection;
and I take every snowflake
as an example
that we are not meant
for indifference
and its coldness,
but gladness
and empathy—
the portrait of a branch
with its starry dust,
like a charcoal sketch
of black on white.

Book of Days

Awaken

I.

Taking the world by the hand,
we lead it as a little child
oft by set example,
washed in prayer
by the Holy Spirit,
secure in the love
of the Father,
restored by the powers
of the Mother,
securely rooted in the Son.

Where the rivers
of faith and countenance
run deep in the spirit being,
there is a place of sustenance
and growth
where all are well-fed at a table
of manna and wine,
professing to be children of faith,
and loving as we are loved.
Halleluiah!

II.

Our Lord, we could never recover
what has been stolen from us by
our enemy; how he placed upon us a yoke—
the years of joy and peace
shattered by false burdens and lies,
burdened by cares of disease
and unrest, sleepless
and unnamed
by those who desired to subjugate
the work of God in us.

All he is has died on a brutal
cross in our soul, if we are taken
captive and beaten, brought down,
maimed and bruised
for what is right in their eyes,
and all leading to death,
for they have ascertained
that we must also die for sin.
We must stretch our hands
in suffering and great pity.

III.

I in this single and solitary cell
have but one purpose:
I have locked myself in the church
that I might serve one God
in absolute dedication
all my years, without fail.
I will be completely alone
as to be completely
with the Lord
in everything.

My worship is both absolute
silence and the screams of horror
at my continued defamation
that seems to plague me to the death,
that of an early grave.
If I had done no wrong,
then I would surely find solace
in the eyes of my Savior,
but my sinful being has refused,
only to declare my innocence in him.

IV.

Sing, O church,
to cover the sounds
of my beating, where I lie
in seclusion: eons away
and yet at your feet.
For I was like Ruth as in days of old,
unlike Miriam I was banished,
and as Deborah, I prophesied to you
as a people called by the Lord
who worship under his anointing.

Dance, people of God
if your feet still move
as if you had not given up
the righteous a long time ago
for a costly meal in the lower realms.
For our Lord was crowned on high
and can have nothing to do
with sorcery and rebellion,
he is averse to anarchy
and the cruel torture of the saints.

V.

The sin of seven generations
could be bound up in one night,
when the prophets of the Lord
come to speak and be heard
by all who would listen.
And the great value of their words
was this: the repression of God's voice in us
leads to illness and disease,
disempowerment and disfigurement,
and even disenfranchisement.

The poor and captives sang
in their chains: I will hope
in the one who was a captive.
Shadows in day
have shut out the light
and I am in anguish within,
but you keep me turning to the rhythm
of your song,
your hands in mine
is what carries me on.

VI.

Some will prophesy to you,
but in your anger
you will eschew them
and spit out their words of fine honey.
For you desired the meat of the gospel,
and would refuse to eat
even the finest of fare
if it were not given to you by the angelic hosts
instead of the mortally wounded
from a sinful generation.

Yet in the castle of the king
this book is revered
as a prophesy among monarchs,
disparate as a debate
between two politicians,
it equivocates both sides
who argue the point of innocence or guilt.
And yet these trappings
of first sin
are as old as Eden,
a tropical garden with a locked gate.

VII.

In this garden, I could eat of the tree of life,
or the tree of good and evil,
and yet I wanted to know
more than God,
and the apple poisoned the ground I walked on.
Suddenly a carnival swept me off the ground
and I was taking a ride on a metal horse,
eating blue cotton candy,
and it stuck in my mouth—
I could no longer speak.

When I realized I had nothing more to say,
my voice became as silent as death,
and many were buried, as the dead increased
in the revelation of the time
of the Madonna of the streets,
who was as a young orchard.
For who would speak, if she said nothing:
yet she was silent as a Madonna with child.
For her time, the thunder crashed,
and rain poured, the snow and hail.
So all of her work was the sacred excellence.

VIII.

The measure of my days
was marked by ceaseless praise
and worry and sighing would flee,
if not bludgeoned from my mind
by those who demanded perfection on earth
and lived in the costly air of new homes
decked in extravagance.
For even poets traded the wealth of earth
for eloquence, and nature spun its paisley song
like a long road of reparation.

Along the road I walked,
only a single nun
from the convent of our Lord—
reading of my prophecy
like a woman wakened
who did not know she was asleep.

IX.

Sing to the Lord,
for he is worthy of praise.
Sing to the Lord,
let the nations praise him.
Lift up your hands with gladness,
let the nations bow.
The horse and rider he has thrown into the sea.
Yahweh has risen in the darkness.
Yahweh had triumphed in the night.
We cry unto you Most Holy.
Our deliverer draweth nigh.

The prophet of the Lord
is singing, and her voice
is heard throughout Israel:
come now, return unto the Lord.
He will bind up the brokenhearted
and heal those wounded in spirit.
Only one God is here today
and speaks through all time—
past, present, and future
of a provision for his sons and daughters
that is not deserved.

X.

We are poor and undeserving,
for how could we work to attain such a thing?
For all our riches and silk garments
are as rags before the king of heaven.
Will you walk with me into the morning
where every tear is a diamond,
and you will wear them like a King.
Will you dance with me into the morning
where rivers fall like an ocean, cleansing
the broken, and I will take you into me.

Desolate woman
have you forgotten
the voice of your freedom?
Who clothed you in scarlet
and marked you "for nothing,"
taking the light from your eyes.
But I am wanting to
feel you alive in my arms
and I was hoping to
dance with you into the night.

Endure

I.

I do not give up the calling that
has drawn me from the first,
but keep first and foremost
the love of my gentle Christ
before me, drawing me, spilling out
his blood, being the sacrifice of great worth.

I keep my eyes fixed
before me on the goal
of being his beloved:
his church, his bride,
clothed in great array,
white as snow, for the world
is steeped in darkness
and grows old with cares.
The seasons pass minute by minute,
year by year, and each a painting
of our Creator's brush,
speaking of the unseen,
providing for the poor,
and I stretch my hands.

II.

The tempest of your greatness
submerges my evil,
restrains my violence,
orders my mayhem,
constructs a temple in my very soul
until I am worth as much as diamonds,
bought at full price.
The days of my youth,
when I could feign madness
are past, and the beauty of darkness stays.

I will only understand you as a child
with no parents,
who eagerly longs for a home
and a place at the table.
You are my family, and
my solitary heart is filled with
the plenty of generous love:
the table is set in my honor
as a long awaited child
now adopted.

III.

You held out your gift
to me of acceptance,
and I receive its embrace
in the place of abandonment.
I was left all alone on a street corner,
and you took my hand,
made me forget the neglect
of poverty and ill-will.
We walk together, a couple
who courts the day.

The denial drains from me
into the ground where I stand,
of all the years I waited
only to be beaten and refused
by a careless husband.
I would become the sea,
the snow, and the rain
to afflict the nation
to the degree to which
I was afflicted,
and then turn and smile.

IV.

Now you love me deeper
than the sun through the forest
needles to wooded floor,
steeping the wildflower meadow
into fine tea.
All manner of wild creatures
understood my cries
of anguish at society's rejection:
to be held at arm's length
is pain behind closed doors.

I am a neutral recipient
of worldly hostility,
the stares, the taunts
and jeers
stole my confidence
that evil be repayed.
So I knew a savage
love who preyed upon
my mind until it broke
and I lay shattered.

V.

The view from the mountaintop
restored my courage
and I sauntered away
a free man with no cares;
I knew everything I wanted
was mine and I let it go.
I am left with only you,
the precious gilt gold
that enamels my prayers
instead of guilt.

I spin tales to the people
who surround me and listen,
I win over the crowd
that once laughed.
They all believe I will
be successful
if I do whatever
suits me best.
But you stand in the background,
doubtful that this is the way.

VI.

My incense rises to the ceiling—
a dense smoke of sandalwood
and jasmine, while I age
with the spiritual journey
that takes me deep into the night
of the soul and back.
I hide from the daylight,
and sleep in the bright hours,
shadows, lengthening
into evening's nocturne.

My eyes are darkened
with lost innocence,
my spirit refuses to be readied,
and my body yearns
for reparation.
I relinquished the people
who stood in my way,
went on alone
for many miles,
and slept in a field.

VII.

The sun set on my anger.
I watched its fiery red
sink into the horizon
beyond the earth,
and I am only human
longing for the divine,
so I reached out and
squeezed from
a pomegranate,
drops of blood.

The fruit fed my heart,
where I hungered
for authentic truth,
the real beyond the false:
children I could call
my own,
who would look for the life
of God in me and call it out,
into full deciduous being,
a rooted tree.

VIII.

The young orchard stirred
within me, of the mystic divine
and its oath.
The trees swayed in the wind.
All I love, I will leave
for the truth of heaven,
all I possess I surrender to the flames;
I take my bag, mount my horse
and ride for the journey
until the journey is done.

As I travelled,
I met both brother and sister,
sun and moon,
the ocean's tide,
and the Madonna of the streets.
She prophesied of this world
and the one to come,
the disasters of the earth
came in her footsteps.
She sought koinonia.

IX.

The community of believers
will again surround the holy saint
in a sacred space.
The Madonna of the streets
will govern both healing
and people without homes.
Their prayers will rise
unafraid,
and their lips will speak of
the promises of a hope
and a future.
With no home or possessions,
they will take the hand of love.

Sparkling gems among the nations,
rubies set in fire,
topaz set in skies,
sapphires set in seas,
emeralds set in mountain green.
Light of day illumines them,
speaks of their power;
and the strength of their martyrdom
among the people is staid, for they
were chosen and remain
faithful to this hour.

X.

My love for you grows deeper
with each day,
yet we remain entranced
so we are interlocked
in our embrace.
When we relinquish our care
it only draws us deeper.
What makes us unable to ever let go,
refusing to sever the bond?

Our yoke plows together
and we know the unity of spirit
from having nothing
but each other.
We will always hold this moment
as the most important
one on earth,
and in the celestial realms,
when we gave up
all for love.

Relinquishment

I.

I said to the Madonna of the streets,
"Your poverty demands my poverty,
all I have is yours;
yet you dwell on high
and decree all the peoples of the spiritual earth,
their times and seasons.
What do you ask of me now?
By holding me with the lightest
touch, your correction is gentle
and your manipulation is kind.
How else would I know where to be?

I see that all I love is in you
and comes from your son;
there is nothing I love here on earth
except what you have given me of heaven,
for I cannot take it there,
and thus despise its burden.
I leave everything behind
to join you in the celestial realms
where the angels worship
and all of creation falls down."

II.

I said to the Madonna of the streets,
"Your sacred work is my preparation,
and you have prepared me since my youth
to work with you,
to participate in your task,
to walk with you on the road everlasting
toward the eternal kingdom.
Your fountain flows in the inner court
where the pool of ivory
is beset by white roses,
and we linger
to rest on the mahogany chaise,
waiting for your presence
to speak.

It is here that we meet with you,
the place of your humble person,
speaking with those you love,
reminding us of the instructions
you have given.

When we are here with you
our souls are satisfied.
Our hearts are open to your heart,
we hear your words of healing."

III.

My tears flow unceasing
in the wake of Christ's death
and crowning life.
For I must give my all
and repent of every sin
of the life of my flesh:
where I forget your humble truth,
fighting with my soul
as I desire to gather all I longed for,
possessions and wealth—
to pour them out before you,
and turn my back.

For I am one to
find what I am searching for,
resuscitate my dying man
or let him die
with the waves of time
breaking over his body.

I am spilled out like broken glass,
unless I repent in tears and face
my martyred self, the streaming blood,
and the goal of paradise.

IV.

I resolve to claim the mystic divine as
my center, the light of my soul
where no darkness can dwell.
I speak of the good of your servants
and renounce disease, illness, and evil.

There is a restless purging in my soul
of all the vices of man,
and I am stormed like a castle wall
by your austerity,
and taken siege.

I no longer own myself,
but belong to greatness
and the end that you
relay as an ultimate destiny.
Your sword slays my bitter self,
full of haughty airs and
deadly poison,
a restless serpent.
I become still,
resonantly calm and humble,
to claim nothing as my own,
to be as the Madonna of the streets
calling her children home.

V.

Where the Madonna of the streets
lays her head
you are the bed on which she rests,
she sleeps in your love
and wakes to your
redemption.

Everything she does
partakes of you,
and so she never grows weary
but walks the miles until day is done.

You are the sweet water
that bathes her soul,
and the ethereal music that
captures her young spirit.

She is covered by your wing
and sleeps under your feathers,
where rest is granted
to her people of the future.

VI.

The Madonna of the streets
is like a seamstress who stitches
and sews to mend a garment
long ago thrown out.

The blue cloth dress
that has been worn for years,
now hangs limply
on the form of a wasted Iris.
Her limbs are white
and her eyes dark.

But when she cried
the Madonna of the streets took the Iris
in her arms,
and gave her a new dress.
This one was velvet
with a beaded bodice, and we did her hair
and put white powder on her face.
Her eyes were lined with coal,
and her lips, red as berries.

The Madonna of the streets sang,
one clear true voice
into the night.

VII.

What could I say to you?
How could I comfort you
except that I reach out to you—
Because I love you.

You will be restored.
You will rise and stand.
You will find your hope again.

Falling like winter's snow
into a pureness not your own
that nothing can separate:
no death, no fear, no shame—
because I love you.

I will restore you to me,
in my love,
in my faithfulness:
here in the valley of sorrow
I will restore you.

VIII.

What sum could repay
the harm done to Iris:
to the one hurt by man,
humanity in its dregs.

The community where he lives
flinches with pain,
his family shows their open wound.

Yet the remorseful
shall open his purse
and pay a dividend
to reimburse suffering.

He shall recompense
the one beaten
to steal her cloak,
disappearing into the night.

What was stolen,
Christ paid for
with great suffering
and anguish of spirit.
Restitution,
hanging on a cross.

IX.

Nourish me
to the core of my being,
strengthen my countenance
and fortify my constitution.

Be the breath of dew
over the cedars of Lebanon,
and the cypress of Syria,
the olive groves of Israel
await your careful cultivation,
and the young orchards of Canada.

The roses in the garden
of reparation are collected
for fine oil, which is bottled
and sold for 33 dollars:
one for every year
until the Savior's death.

The great lion roars
and I am safe,
for he has triumphed over the eagle,
and bears the coat of arms.

X.

Dust of our eyes,
unquenched land,
with fearful hearts
and trembling hands,
we were the blind,
we were the lame,
but one day we will see again.

We shall see,
we shall hear,
water in the wilderness,
the redeemed shall walk here.

Barren of hope
we leave the dead,
in streams of light
we bow our heads,
upon the way we will return
and ransomed we shall sing in Zion.

Book of Tears

The Crushed Rose

I.

Never have I seen such stain
as that which marred us forever
for the eternal.
Never have I seen such sainthood
as that which flowed
from the blood upon the tree.
Such glory emanated
from his face, that
he was no human, but divine.
Who crushed the rose of my heart
to produce such sweet fragrance?

Such celestial beings
have I not understood until this time,
their fluttering breath
and baited wing.
Angels rest their heads
upon my shoulder;
the cherubims' eyes
blink unceasingly,
and the archangels shimmer before
the throne of my heart.

II.

Here you are,
both now and forever,
innocent of wrong, and perfect
as a bridegroom waiting for his bride,
the wedding feast,
the celebration of life:
the things that last forever,
and the Madonna of the streets
has not despaired.

You were a peasant king,
born into the hovels of poverty,
yet she anointed you with the oils
of frankincense and myrrh
to consummate
your death and burial—
as the transcendence of
all you came to be
and have given your soul to find:
the lost sheep of Israel,
the budding olive branch.
She bears the budding staff
in her fragile arms,
the portrait of true
stability and knowledge.

III.

We chant in the voices of old
our song rises, pure and true,
chastising us to live
as servants of the mystic divine:
to rise from the dead
as you rose,
your death to sin
in us
incarnate, and having
power beyond
the grave.

The Madonna of the streets
sits in the chapel
beyond the wrought iron gate,
steeped in heady incense,
her heart,
now inspired with our prayers
in seclusion,
those who have promised
their dedication
to the one
they love more
than this world.

IV.

What I have waited for all my life
has come to be: I am a bride
and he is my magnificent anointed one;
the step upon the stair of time,
a prince of the sun and moon,
the wind and rain, the planets
and constellations—all bow down
and worship his finery: fire, earth,
metal, wood, water, and air.
His strength is like that
of a thousand horses to defend us,
his river of love flows
clear as crystal.
The Alpha and Omega,
both first and last
among spirits and men:
all will find their wholeness
in his perfection
for their own imperfection.

The Madonna bowed her head,
interceding for the poor,
caring for the weak,
feeding the hungry.

V.

"Sing," said the Madonna.
"Let the earth rejoice
that it is no longer
under the dominion
of evil, the darkness
does not reign
unpierced by love,
the stars glisten
as a martyr's tears
and here the truth of life
is spoken: go deeper, deeper."

She speaks of revelation,
not an afterword,
or an afterthought,
but a journey
that bids one
depart at once
for a far-away land.
Here one must
wrest the soul
from its enchantment
and tell it, "Fight!"

VI.

There is a battle
for one's eternal soul
and one must take
his portion, his cup
and willingly, his vow.
Whoever one serves shall love
or betray him,
seduce or invite him,
accuse or deliver him,
condemn or acquit him,
possess or relinquish him.

The Madonna speaks of love incarnate:
where there is hatred, let envy cease,
and empathy resound in the lives
of those trained for war,
who swear their allegiance
to the end,
who are men of violence,
yet love with compassion.
They will never forget
that our greatest freedom
came at the cost of bloodshed:
the blood rose.

VII.

The war of her angels in heaven
and on earth
has overthrown
the evil one, and he languishes
waiting for his eternal doom;
those who love his ego
will swear at life's injustice,
will waste every resource,
will become pale with fear
at their wicked poison:
creating trash words
where there once was verse,
and calling art uninspired.

Yet Christ is as a statue from marble,
that stands in the greatest
museum on earth.
No man can touch his face.
Even Michelangelo's David
cannot rival his perfection,
his chiseled brow and deep set eyes;
his love, like an oil painting
in the Louvre,
never to be abandoned
or forgotten.

Truce

I.

My heart crumbled beneath
this red and white truce
with the Madonna of the streets.
My Creator wanted
my absolute devotion,
and the length of my years,
days, hours, minutes, and seasons
were my eternal gift,
my journey into the mystic divine:
my spiritual path of all seasons
despite the shifting shadows of human nature.

I was one to have no children,
to be of solitude and contemplation,
to take my vows of poverty,
chastity, enclosure, and obedience.
I rise every day in repentance and to pray;
I sleep with the fervor of grace
echoing in my bones.
I see the message of the sun and moon,
the dance of constellations,
and interpret their meanings
like those of foreigners, speaking in tongues.

II.

The universal street
is where human beings,
their whims, values, and vices
are played out for their own good,
the good of others, or the benefit
of the mystic divine for eternity.
All at once, my black and white factual mind
became the meldings of a stained glass window,
the color rich and sunlight streaming
to illumine me
with understanding not my own:
there was a woman with long dark hair
standing unbidden in the shadows.

I walk the halls of this small unknown
convent, covered from head to toe
in the robe of a nun,
yet the language of verse
struck a ringing brass note,
and sheathed me with the dress
of humanity from every culture.
This was a poetry that came
from the weathered beach,
like gathering seashells
that are beautiful and unusual.

III.

The ringing thunder over the shore
had a voice of its own, prophesying.

The Madonna of the streets
carried a staff, and her long dark hair
was bound by a red scarf.
She lived in simplicity and owned nothing,
enduring by the work of her hands.
Her skin was washed by the salt
of the seashore.

On the inside
she was a country waiting
for deliverance;
on the outside she was stately
at her innocence.
She waited to bear the holy one.
She knew the sanctity
and the sacredness of
gathering her soul to birth
and rebirth throughout the ages.
Holy mother, come
now deliver us
with the gift of your son.

IV.

We said to this woman
who had espoused poverty:
"Healing to all peoples
comes through your offspring,
and you are
the Lady of Guadalupe.
Where once you were
like a queen in a castle,
now you walk the streets
with your face hidden
by your hair,
looking for the children
of your heart.

The peace of nations is in
your very robe, the tree
for their healing grows in your garden,
and sin is assuaged
by your merciful face.
I will wait in silence
until the prayers you give me
are of the divine nature, not my own.
Until they are as lace,
covering the countryside,
and I gather them like wildflowers."

V.

"I have no other treasure than that
which is produced by my heart in yours,
the mother of those without homes.
The mystery of the divine
cannot be answered
in words alone, but the words that
unselfconsciously lead to prayer.
I hope this will lead you
to the water of the living stream,
and will quench the thirst of your soul
in a modern and inconvenienced world.

The world
did not have time
for a "little Christ,"
it was necessary
to make him big
and commercial
and important enough
to earn both money and riches.
Yet he was poor,
and despises not our poverty
and the value of hard work."

VI.

May I never
be feared of the shadows,
and the Madonna of the streets
who called me to the mystic divine
in the first place,
and emptied my wants,
desires, and wealth
for a person I could not see—
and yet I trust implicitly.
May I never revoke
my lifetime vows
in the convent of our Lord.

May I never die
and only lie in a graveyard
of a small town
in British Columbia,
but carry on the work in dedication
to the mystic divine forever in eternity.
My words will stand only
if they are measured by his own,
and the lessons I've learned
in both despair and consternation
reflect Christ's perfection and peace.

VII.

What I have won by the world,
aside from the simple purpose,
I have lost in heaven,
and to this day I know only of
the emptying of everything
that would hold me back
from taking her cup
and drinking the wine.
What I cannot take
with me I now cut free,
breaking the bread.

The trappings of pain and guilt
are left like a chrysalis from which
I have emerged the butterfly.
He who once died,
now dies in me.
He who once rose,
now rises in me.
And the nectar is pungent.
I am freedom: and where I walk,
all who follow will taste its sweetness.

Book of Years

Love Shall Burn

I.

Her song broke the sky right at the beginning,
and all that was wintered and frozen
began to melt under the great tree of time;
the new green life unpeeled itself
beneath stormy skies
and grew in shoots of living breath,
each colored flower rimmed with dew
spoke of the mystic divine surrounding
a woman that hand-picked their warm hues,
and water colored each one.

The rain beat down,
edifying her work, filling
the depths with new waters
and here there was an abundance
of life; waiting for her story to begin,
the lives of creatures
both great and small
to chronicle their being
in a timeline of pleasant days
and healing's hundredfold
blessings to the earth
and its poverty.

II.

What could love taste
besides her fragrant orchard
of fresh bloom,
opening in the new sun,
spilling its blossoms
like rain over the ground.
The cherry, plum, and apple trees
give forth their promise
of new life, being bearers
of prophecy in the very grove
their cultivator once stood
and contemplated with all his heart,
saying:

"This young orchard of promise
will bear much fruit,
and will be a dividend of plenty;
the wind will blow
in the arms of its branches
and its pink and white
sanctity shall be reminiscent
of youth, when not yet in its prime."

III.

And the duress of rain and storm
did not shake the perfumed grove,
for its cultivator was a wise man
and carefully, he tended his orchard.
The summer came with its warmth,
and the apples grew magenta and shiny,
rounded and juicy, tempting
those who knew of such a place.

The fruit of the orchard was harvested
and each barrel of bright-hued sweetness
was a tribute to the owner who
had paid the price
and purchased the orchard.

He always believed that
it would not be to his detriment
to have a stock of such delicious fruit
to fill his pantry and root cellar
for winter months.
For what is more pleasing than the crunch
of a juice apple in midwinter,
a dried cherry in burgundy,
or the warmth of a stewed plum?

IV.

The children of the cultivator
grew with the magical fruit from the orchard,
and it gave them promise
so that they were red-cheeked and hearty,
picking cherries to eat in the summertime,
apples in the fall, burnished and bright,
and supping on warm plums in the winter.

The youngest girl would sit beneath the trees,
reading books that would rivet her for hours—
until she was well-read.
When she had read every book she could
lay her eyes on, she began to write her own book,
using many pages of lined white paper
to complete the task.

She had become a young woman,
the day she found the book
she had written as a child, and decided it should
tell the story of the orchard to everyone.
She sent it away, and called it
"The Young Orchard."

V.

"The Young Orchard"
was published and made into a book
many years ago.
Some have read it, although
today, many have not.
For if they read it,
they would recognize the old orchard
at the end of Mission Road—
there are the ruins of an old house,
the rose garden, where
a few silver petals reside,
and the shadows.

The trees still stand in decorum,
their blossoms still shed
their papery blooms over
the hard earth, but
the fruit falls to the ground,
unnoticed.

The children no longer play
in its reaches,
for they have grown up
and gone away many years ago.

VI.

When I was a young woman,
I would sit under the plum tree
and contemplate for long hours
while shadows grew long
across the vegetable garden
with its bean stalks and dreamy rows of corn.

What become of my journey into the self today,
one only knows if the mystic divine
hath found me—I grew up and went away also,
and the whisperings of the old garden
may have almost forgotten.

I decided to travel to foreign lands,
knowing the places I would visit
could bring significance to my dreams
and fulfillment to my prayers,
for the steeping of my soul and a fire
over injustice that would evoke change.
A shepherd had said to me once,
"I hope to never quench the fire of your spirit."
So I went into the world with my body
and when I found its innocence crucified,
I left my life and title,
then went to live among the poor.

VII.

The ebony face watched me, standing
in the door of her hut,
bright dress wrapped
around her in shades of African desert,
intrigued with my presence
where the heat doesn't relent, as fiery hunger
pounding away the grain with a rock
until it is milled like fine dark powder.

If I had been collecting only rooibos tea
from the dark continent,
I would have left and returned home;
but I was collecting hearts
so I stayed to carefully observe
what I was not to change,
but value as tradition
from one generation to the next.

VIII.

I carefully fingered
the banana leaf baskets,
the carved wood bowls,
the thin white raiment
that made clothing for
under the hot sun.

And then I saw her:
a Madonna with child,
carrying the poor
beneath her cloak.

Her baby cried out,
and she nursed him
without any fear
of not having enough food to eat.

So he slept in the
grass hut, and when
his hands grew into a man's
he became a cultivator
of the plantation.

IX.

One day I know that children
will not die of hunger when there is food;
I know that where there is food
children still die of hunger.

But there is a mother
who feeds her hungry,
spooning to their mouths
the food of the spirit.

She is found in every country
and every nation,
a multi-national voice
that rises from the dust of the desert.

Those who contemplate her child
and his purpose on earth
have begun to enter
the nourishment of the mystic divine.

X.

For the requiem
of Afghanistan,
or the lament of India,
to the desert melody of the Sahara,
or the cadence suns
of Saudi Arabia.
Beneath the nocturnal spires of London,
broken like bread
and wine of the Parisian waltz,
from the ringing domes
of the Basilica in Rome,
and the singing balconies of Spain,
harmonic moon rising round and full
over foreign isles.

Day by day we are learning
more and more
when we turn and thank
the cultivator of our love.

In this sun-drenched place
under the sky
where truth is not relinquished
at the cost of human life,
love shall burn.